GW00649678

Airlife
England

Acknowledgements

Since most of my own photographs of this period are black and white I was able to go out and renew old acquaintances and raid a number of slide collections. This gave me the difficult task of picking out from several hundred slides what was not to be used. My thanks for pictures used go to Ian Keast (IDK), Peter Whalley (CPW), Steve Williams (SGW) and most especially to Ken Fielding (KVF). The latter's collection and fund of airline stories could fill several books. Thanks also to Keith Crowden for assorted text facts.

Copyright © 2000 Gerry Manning

First published in the UK in 2000
by Airlife Publishing Ltd

British Library Cataloguing-in-Publication Data
A catalogue record for this book
is available from the British Library

ISBN 1 84037 124 2

Typeset by Rowland Phototypesetting Ltd,
Bury St Edmunds, Suffolk.
Printed in Hong Kong

Airlife Publishing Ltd

101 Longden Road, Shrewsbury, SY3 9EB,
England
E-mail: airlife@airlifebooks.com
Website: www.airlifebooks.com

Contents

Introduction

The basic premise of this book is to illustrate a range of both airlines and airliners that operated during the decade of the 1960s. It of course cannot be complete as it is of limited size. It was a time of change, for despite the introduction of the jet airliner in the 1950s with such types as the Comet and the Boeing 707, the year 1960 was one in which piston power was still the most common form of propulsion for a passenger aeroplane. By the end of the following ten years even the holiday charter carriers were changing to jets or at least turbo props.

What I have attempted to do with the captions is to note who the carrier was or still is, what the aeroplane type was and where the picture was taken. Finally to list the fate of that particular aircraft.

The enthusiasts of today, be they spotters or photographers, who were not born when the pictures were taken, will notice that the biggest difference to today's civil airports is that of access. Almost every location had a good public viewing area or balcony within close proximity of the aircraft. This was not a bad thing since few people had the range of cameras and telephoto lenses that are taken for granted today. Nor was the use of colour slides or prints as widespread: lots of photographers spent those years with black and white film in their cameras.

Gerry Manning
Liverpool

Channel Airways was a UK independent carrier which assumed that name in 1956, having flown since 1946 as East Anglian Flying Services. It flew both charter and scheduled services until its demise in February 1972, by which time the fleet had included BAC1-11s, Comets and Tridents. Seen here at Liverpool Speke, in August 1965, is Vickers Viscount 701 G-AMOH (c/n 21) on lease to British Eagle to operate the London flight. This aircraft was sold on to Cambrian and withdrawn from use at the end of 1971 in Cardiff where it was broken up the following year. (IDK)

Beirut, Lebanon is the home of **MEA – Middle East Airlines** which from 1945 to this day has flown scheduled passenger services to many locations. Vickers Viscount 745D OD-ADD (c/n 243) is pictured with passengers disembarking at Jerusalem in March 1967. The aeroplane was sold in Africa and carried a number of registrations. It was operated up to the mid-1990s by Trans Service Airlift of Kinshasa in the Democratic Republic of Congo. (CPW)

SE-CNK Vickers Viscount 745D (c/n 227) of Swedish carrier **Falconair** is seen at Liverpool Speke, October 1967. The Malmo-based company had begun charter operations in May of that year with three Viscounts. The company ceased operations in September 1970. This airframe was withdrawn from use at Malmo during 1970 and broken up two years later. (IDK)

LEFT:
Sywell in Northamptonshire saw the birth of **Treffield Aviation** in September 1965 with two Avro 19 Ansons. The company name was derived from one of the founders, Lord Trefgarne. The life of the carrier was short, lasting just under two years and closing down in June 1967. Vickers Viscount 812 G-ATVE (c/n 366) is seen following maintenance by British Eagle at Liverpool Speke in the month the airline ceased trading. This aircraft was returned from its lease to Channel Airways, withdrawn from use in 1969 and broken up in 1972. (KVF)

RIGHT:
This wonderful night shot at Bordeaux in August 1964 shows **British Eagle** Vickers Viscount 701 G-AMOO (c/n 28). This carrier was in its day perhaps the finest of all the UK independents, flying both scheduled and charter passenger services. The airline started flying in 1948 and operated for twenty years until December 1968. This aircraft moved on to Cambrian Airways, was withdrawn from use at the end of 1970 and scrapped the following year. (KVF)

BELOW:
Austrian Airlines is that country's flag carrier being founded during 1958 in Vienna. Services are flown to many locations world-wide with a fleet that includes the latest wide-body Airbus designs. Seen here is Vickers Viscount 837 OE-LAL (c/n 441) on a service to Manchester Ringway in June 1965. The aircraft had been delivered new in 1960 and was sold to a Colombian operator in 1971. It was damaged beyond repair in that country in December 1977. (KVF)

Photographed at London Gatwick in August 1968 is Vickers Viscount 812 G-AVNJ (c/n 361) of British independent airline **Air Ferry**. This carrier flew holiday charter operations from 1963 to October 1968 from its base in Manston, Kent. This aircraft was withdrawn in October 1969 being scrapped during 1972. (GM)

Founded during 1937 as Trans-Canada Airlines in Montreal the company was renamed **Air Canada** in 1964. This carrier is today one of that country's two major airlines with services both domestic and international. Seen at Calgary AL is Vickers Viscount 757 CF-THB (c/n 219) on an internal flight in June 1967. The aircraft was withdrawn at Teulon MN in 1975 and later broken up. (KVF)

Lufthansa is the German flag carrier, being founded in 1926, and taking its current form in 1955. Operations are flown world-wide as well as internally. Vickers Viscount 819 D-ANAC (c/n 370) is seen at Frankfurt Rhein Main in June 1962. The fate of this aircraft was to be sold first to Israel and then to the UK where it spent its last few years as a cabin crew trainer at Southend Airport. It was scrapped in 1993. (CPW)

BEA – British European Airways was the government-owned carrier covering domestic and European scheduled passenger services. The airline was formed following World War II in 1946, and was the first operator of a turbine-powered aircraft when, in June 1950, a Vickers Viscount operated a service from London to Paris. Illustrated is Viscount 802 G-AOHM (c/n 162) at Manchester Ringway in August 1964 in the colour scheme most associated with the operator. In 1974 the airline was merged with BOAC to form British Airways who are today one of the world's leading and most profitable carriers. This aeroplane flew on and at the time of writing is still operational as a freighter in South Africa, having only left British skies in the early part of 1998. (IDK)

Liverpool-based **Starways** was a passenger carrier which operated both scheduled and charter flights. Seen here at base in May 1963 are two of the airline's fleet. In the foreground is Vickers Viscount 707 G-APZB (c/n 30) and beyond it is Douglas DC-3 Dakota G-AMPY (c/n 26569). The operator was taken over by British Eagle in 1964. The fate of the aeroplanes was that the Viscount ended its days at Southend where it was stored from 1968 until being scrapped two years later. The Dakota is still operated as a pollution control spray aircraft in the care of Air Atlantique at Coventry in the UK. (IDK)

British independent **Cambrian Airlines** was based in Cardiff, South Wales and from its start in 1935 it grew to be a respected scheduled passenger carrier. It was taken over by British Airways in 1972 thus losing its identity. Vickers Viscount 701 G-ALWF (c/n 5) is at Liverpool Speke in June 1966 on a regular passenger service, one of many flown from this location. This airframe is the oldest Viscount to survive and after a period of preservation at Liverpool it was moved by road to Duxford Museum to join a number of other classic airliners on view to the public. (CPW)

BUA – British United Airlines was founded by the merger of no less than eight airlines in 1960. It flew for ten years operating both passenger, freight, charter and scheduled services before being purchased by Caledonian to form British Caledonian. Vickers Viscount 833 G-APTB (c/n 424) is seen on a rare visit to Liverpool Speke in July 1966. The aircraft was sold to Arkia – Israel Inland Airways in October 1969 and was destroyed in a night training flight a couple of weeks later. (KVF)

The Hungarian state-owned flag carrier **Malev** flew this Ilyushin 14P into Liverpool Speke in March 1966 direct from Prague. Its passengers were the football team 'Honved' who were due to play Liverpool. This aircraft HA-MAD (c/n 14803028) is a licensed-built aircraft, being one of 80 manufactured by VEB at Dresden in what was then East Germany. The IL-14 was a direct development of the Soviet Union's first post-war transport aircraft, the IL-12. First flown in 1950 the IL-14 entered service in 1954 with both Aeroflot and the Soviet Air Force. It had a longer range than the IL-12 but carried less passengers. Power was provided by two Shvetsov ASh-82 air-cooled radial piston engines of 1900 horse power driving a four bladed propeller. This airframe no longer exists. (KVF)

Aer Lingus – Irish International Airlines has flown scheduled passenger services to European and American destinations since 1936. It flew a service from Dublin to Liverpool throughout World War II. In 1951 it was the third operator to order the Vickers Viscount, putting the type into service in 1954. EI-AKL Viscount 808 (c/n 423) is seen at Manchester Ringway in August 1964. It was sold on to the Sultan of Oman's Air Force in 1973 and then on to operators in Africa where it was withdrawn and stored in 1984 at Kinshasa and then later broken up. (IDK)

Spanish charter operator **Aviaco – Aviacion y Comercio SA** is a subsidiary of Iberia, being founded in 1948. Over the years the airline has flown thousands of holiday makers to and from the sunspots of Spain and does so to this day. Palma Majorca, September 1965, is the location of Douglas DC-4 EC-ACF (c/n 42988). This popular type was the backbone of many charter operators during the 1960s. It was powered by four Pratt & Whitney R2000 radial piston engines of 1450hp each. This aircraft was sold to British Air Ferries at the end of 1972 and broken up for spares the following year. (KVF)

G-ARIY Douglas C-54D Skymaster (c/n 3116) of UK independent **Starways** is seen at its Liverpool Speke base on new year's day 1964, the day the carrier was taken over by British Eagle. This aircraft was not taken into the British Eagle fleet and was passed on to the airport fire service who were able to use it until the mid-1970s, by which time it had been burnt beyond recognition. (KVF)

TOP RIGHT:
ACE Freighters (Aviation Charter Enterprises) was Europe's first all-cargo airline. Operations started in March 1964 from its Gatwick base. The carrier mainly flew Lockheed Constellations (see picture) but had two Douglas Skymasters in its fleet. G-APEZ DC-4 (c/n 42921) is seen devoid of engines at Coventry in September 1968, having been withdrawn from service two years earlier. The aircraft was scrapped at this location. ACE went into liquidation and ceased operations in September 1966. (IDK)

LEFT:
British Independent carrier **Invicta** was formed in November 1964 at Manston in Kent. The airline flew holiday charter flights and a scheduled service between its base and Ostend in Belgium. G-ASPN (c/n 10337) Douglas C-54A Skymaster is seen at Liverpool Speke in February 1965. It was to end its days in Africa, being withdrawn from use in Kinshasa, Republic of Congo in 1996. Invicta's first life ended when services ceased in October 1975 due to financial problems. This was short-lived, as in the following December a new company, Invicta International, started services with two Bristol Britannias and this continued until 1981. (KVF)

RIGHT:

Dan-Air's name was derived from the shipping broker owners Davis and Newman. It was formed in 1953 and at one time was the largest independent airline in Europe. The airline flew passenger and freight flights on both scheduled and charter operations. In November 1992 the airline, being in financial difficulties, was taken-over by British Airways. G-APID Douglas C-54D Skymaster (c/n 10408) is seen at Liverpool Speke in May 1965. Two years later it was sold in Spain where it was eventually withdrawn from use and became a snack bar at Seville. It was later broken up. (KVF)

Zurich-based Swiss charter operator **Balair** was a leading ITC (Inclusive Tour Charter) operator owned by the national flag carrier Swissair. It was merged with Geneva-based CTA (Compagnie de Transport Aerien), also owned by the same carrier, to fly as Balair CTA. HB-ILU Douglas C-54E Skymaster (c/n 27289) is at Liverpool Speke in September 1965. This aircraft flew on for many more years in various parts of the world and has now ended its flying days at Frankfurt Rhein Main, back in its original United States Army Air Force markings, preserved as a memorial to the Berlin Airlift. (KVF)

UK independent **British Eagle** obtained two Skymasters from Saudi Arabian Airlines in 1964 to operate its holiday charter programme. G-ASPM Douglas C-54B (c/n 10543) is at its home base of Liverpool Speke in July of that year. This aircraft ended its days in Africa, being reported withdrawn from use at Kinshasa, Republic of Congo as late as 1996. (KVF)

Air Ferry was a UK charter carrier based at Manston in Kent. Operations commenced at the end of March 1963 with a fleet of two Vickers Vikings and a single Skymaster. These were kept busy on holiday charters but the company also flew cross-channel scheduled services to Le Touquet (France) and Ostend (Belgium). At the end of 1964 the airline was bought out by the Air Holdings Group which continued to operate the company as Air Ferry until the end of the 1968 season when the carrier was merged into British United. G-ASFY Douglas C-54A Skymaster (c/n 10335) is seen on a wet February day in 1965 at Liverpool Speke. This aircraft was sold to Lavco in 1969 and ten years later was withdrawn and broken up in Malta. (KVF)

Irish passenger charter and freight company **Aer Turas** was formed in Dublin during 1962 and continues to operate to this day. EI-APK Douglas DC-4 Skymaster (c/n 42911) is seen at Wymeswold in March 1967 receiving maintenance from Fields before the start of the summer holiday season. Named *Monarch of Munster* this aircraft ended its days on the fire dump at Hal Far, Malta in 1983 and was scrapped two years later. (IDK)

Visiting Vienna, in July 1968, is **MEA – Middle East Airlines** Sud-Est S.E.210 Caravelle VI.N OD-AEE (c/n 153). The Beirut-based carrier flew to many European locations as well as routes in the middle east. This aircraft had a short life with a spectacular end. It was delivered in March 1964 and on 28 December 1968 was destroyed when Israeli commandos attacked Beirut airport. (SGW)

The French national flag carrier **Air France** was the largest operator of the Caravelle. The airline missed the chance however of being the first operator when it was beaten by one week by SAS who flew the inaugural flight from Copenhagen to Beirut in April 1959. F-BJTN Sud-Est S.E.210 Caravelle III (c/n 145) is seen at Liverpool Speke, January 1967, after being diverted from a weather-closed Manchester. The aircraft was sold to Air Cambodge and destroyed in an attack by communist guerrillas on Phnom Penh in January 1971. (IDK)

Rome-based Italian holiday charter operator **SAM – Societa Aerea Mediterranea** was owned by Alitalia. The attractive colours were seen at many UK airports as the airline flew hundreds of charter flights. In 1974 the carrier was merged into its parent company. I-DABT Sud-Est S.E.210 Caravelle VI-N (c/n 85) is seen at London Gatwick in June 1969. The aircraft ended its days with the same carrier when it was withdrawn from service in 1978 and later scrapped. (KVF)

Seen arriving at Paris Orly in June 1963 is OE-LCE Sud-Est S.E.210 Caravelle VI-R (c/n 156) of the Austrian national carrier **Austrian Airlines** on a regular scheduled flight. The Caravelles had replaced Viscounts (see picture) on most routes and were themselves supplanted by Douglas DC-9s from the middle of 1972. This aircraft ended its days in Quito, Ecuador, where it was used for spares during 1978. (CPW)

LEFT:
RAM – Royal Air Maroc is the government-owned flag carrier based in Casablanca, the capital of Morocco. The fact that France was the former colonial power no doubt had a strong influence on RAM to purchase the Caravelle. The design entered service with the carrier in May 1960. CN-CCV Sud-Est S.E.210 Caravelle III (c/n 32) is seen here at Marseille Marignane in August 1964. The aircraft was destroyed in a crash whilst on approach to Casablanca in April 1970. (CPW)

ABOVE:
Emerald Airways was a Belfast, Northern Ireland-based carrier formed in July 1965. Scheduled services were operated from base to Prestwick (Scotland) as well as domestic flights. In November 1966 the airline was taken over by Dublin-based Hibernian Airways who bought a 55% share. Following the demise of the major shareholder in October 1967, Emerald was put into liquidation during December of that year. EI-APJ Douglas DC-3 Dakota (c/n 33042) is seen at Prestwick, May 1967. The fate of this aircraft was to be reduced to spares in Lagos, Nigeria following an accident in 1981. (IDK)

RIGHT:
The Douglas DC-3 was and still is the greatest of the workhorse props. The design has seen off many post-war 'Dakota replacements' and proved that the only Dakota replacement is another Dakota. G-AKNB (c/n 9043) is in the colours of UK independent carrier **British United** at Blackpool in May 1966. As expected, this airframe is still current but is now in America. (IDK)

British independent carrier **Derby Airways** was based at that town's airport, Burnaston (now a Toyota car factory). It flew scheduled passenger services and holiday charters to European destinations. During 1964 the company changed its name to British Midland which has become one of the UK's leading domestic and European airlines. Douglas DC-3 Dakota G-ANTD (c/n 26414) is at base in August 1964. It was withdrawn from use in 1973 and broken up. (IDK)

ABOVE:
Seen here at Tripoli, Libya in February 1969 is Douglas DC-3 Dakota N484F (c/n 9470) of **Lavco – Libyan Aviation Company** – a Benghazi-based carrier which supported the country's large oil industry. This aircraft suffered the indignity of being used as target practice by the Libyan army during 1979. (KVF)

BELOW:
Wales-based **Cambrian Airways** was one of the most regular carriers to fly into Liverpool Speke. G-AGHS Douglas DC-3 Dakota (c/n 10099) is seen here during February 1967. It was sold two years later to a company in Cyprus and ended its days after being withdrawn from use at Beirut where its registration was cancelled in 1976. (IDK)

Dublin was the base of **Hibernian Airlines**. It was formed in 1966 and operated ad hoc passenger and freight charters. Financial problems caused the demise of the company in October of the following year. EI-APB Douglas DC-3 Dakota (c/n 25600) is seen at Liverpool Speke in May 1966. This aircraft was scrapped at Prestwick in 1969 and was put on the fire dump. (KVF)

Irelfly was a UK charter company based at Shoreham and Gatwick which came and went during one year. Founded in January 1966 it ceased all services in November of the same year. G-AMSH Douglas DC-3 Dakota (c/n 33331) is seen on a charter to Liverpool Speke in July 1966. This aircraft operated until 1978 in the Yemen when it was withdrawn from use. (KVF)

British scheduled and charter carrier **Dan-Air** operated four Dakotas. The airline obtained the first in 1953 and flew them until the last was withdrawn in 1970. Seen at Liverpool Speke in August 1964 is G-AMSS (c/n 32840). This aircraft was sold in Iran and eventually was cancelled from the register. (IDK)

Channel Airways operated nine Dakotas during its operational life, acquiring them between 1960 and 1962. The last one was withdrawn from use in March 1970. G-AHCV Douglas DC-3 Dakota (c/n 12443) is seen at Southend, May 1967, following the end of its service life. It was broken up at this location at the start of 1970. (IDK)

Based in Antwerp, Belgium, **Delta Air Transport** first flew Dakotas in 1968 and ended the type association in 1972 when they were replaced by Convairs. This company operates today as DAT – Belgian Regional, flying a large number of international services around Europe. Seen at London Gatwick in June 1968 is OO-VDF (c/n 9410). The aeroplane was last reported as stored at Entebbe, Uganda at the end of 1996. (IDK)

Westpoint Aviation was founded in the south-west of England at Exeter in 1961. It operated passenger and freight charters on an ad hoc basis. 'British' was added to the airline's name during 1963. The carrier was put into liquidation in May 1966. Seen following that demise is G-ALYF Douglas DC-3 Dakota (c/n 19350) at Liverpool Speke in June 1966. The aircraft was dismantled at Prestwick in 1967 and used for rescue training at Abbotsinch during 1971. Its last claim to fame was as a prop in the Yorkshire Television series 'Airline' in 1981. (KVF)

ABOVE:
1958 saw the start of **Martin's Air Charter**, which was based in the Dutch city of Amsterdam and flew charter operations. The name Martinair was adopted in 1974 and today the carrier flies long-haul operations using wide-body jets such as Boeing 747s and MD-11s. They are owned by KLM. June 1964 saw this Douglas DC-3 Dakota PH-MAB (c/n 4500) at Liverpool Speke. This aircraft moved on to the Indonesian Navy in 1970 and although withdrawn from service was believed to be still in existence at Surabaya as late as 1994. (KVF)

BELOW:
British independent **Starways** operated Dakotas from 1950 until it was taken over by British Eagle at the end of 1963. DC-3 G-AMSN (c/n 33379) is seen at its Liverpool base days after the airline closed. The aircraft has had a number of owners and registrations but has found its way back to the UK where it can still be found. (KVF)

Norwegian scheduled carrier **Widerøe** flew two Dakotas from its Oslo base to locations in the north of that country. Charter operations also flew such things as a complete ship's crew to port cities. LN-RTE (c/n 11697) is seen on such an operation unloading its passengers in July 1964 at Liverpool Speke. The airline still runs services to this day, having a fleet of over twenty de Havilland (Canada) DHC-8 Dash 8 commuters. This pictured aircraft was withdrawn from use and used for fire practice at Oslo in 1971. (KVF)

Supporting Libya's oil industry from Tripoli was this **Linair – Libyan National Airways** Douglas DC-3 Dakota OO-CBX (c/n 33224), at base in March 1969. The company was formed by Belgian flag carrier Sabena and various oil companies. The operations, both scheduled domestic and charters, continued from 1962 to 1973 when the aircraft were sold. This aircraft had a number of subsequent owners and was reported cancelled from the civil register of the Dominican Republic in 1981. (KVF)

LEFT:
Fairways was a Dutch charter company based at Rotterdam. Two Dakotas were used for the company start up in 1961. Martin's Air Charter took over the carrier in 1964. PH-SCC (c/n 19458) is seen on a charter operation to Liverpool Speke in December 1964. This aircraft was last noted on the Venezuelan register in 1989. (KVF)

BELOW:
British independent **Dan-Air** had a huge fleet of Comets, covering the 4/4B/4C models, over forty were owned by the company but not all were put into service. Seen here at London Gatwick, April 1969, is de Havilland DH-106 Comet 4 G-APDP (c/n 6417). It was withdrawn from service in 1973 and then sold on to the Royal Aircraft Establishment at Farnborough who used it for a further two years. It was not until 1984 that the aircraft was finally scrapped. (KVF)

Kuwait Airways, the national flag carrier founded in 1954, bought two new Comets, that were delivered in 1963 and 1964. Scheduled flights were made to London Heathrow, where de Havilland DH-106 Comet 4C 9K-ACE (c/n 6474) is seen in March 1964. The airline is still current today operating a fleet of Boeing and Airbus wide-bodies. This Comet was sold to Dan-Air in 1971. The airline operated it until 1977 and it was broken up the following year. (KVF)

BELOW:
Malmo-based **Transair Sweden** was formed in 1951 with three Airspeed Consuls to fly newspapers. The fleet mix over the years has included DC-3/C-46/DC-6s. The airline was best known as a holiday charter operator but it did fly some scheduled services on behalf of SAS. Operations ceased in 1981. Seen on an operation to London Gatwick in August 1968 is Douglas DC-7B SE-ERL (c/n 45346). It was withdrawn from service and scrapped the following year at the company base. (GM)

Danish charter operator **InterNord** flew both Danish and Swedish registered aircraft until its demise at the end of 1968. Seen at London Gatwick in August of that year is OY-ANA Douglas DC-7B (c/n 45402). The aircraft pictured was broken up in 1973 at Nimes, France. (GM)

Spanish charter operator **TASSA** (Trabajeros Aereos del Sahara SA) like many operators of its day flew the big four engine Douglas types on holiday flights around Europe. EC-AVP Douglas DC-7 (c/n 44289) is seen on the ramp at Palma Majorca in September 1965. The carrier had been wound up three months prior to this. The aircraft was stored at this location until 1970 and then scrapped. (KVF)

Spantax was a Spanish charter line based on the island of Majorca. The airline was formed in October 1959 to fly contracts for the oil industry in Spanish Morocco. It was instrumental in setting up Air Mauritanie with both aircraft and crew. 1963 saw the acquisition of a pair of DC-7s for holiday charter work. This continued with a variety of types until 1988 when services were suspended. The fleet was a common sight at many European airports as it flew holidaymakers to Palma and other Spanish destinations. EC-ATR Douglas DC-7C (c/n 45309) is at Manchester Ringway in August 1964. This aircraft has been preserved and is located in the Canary Islands. (IDK)

Copenhagen was the base for charter operator and I/T (inclusive tour) carrier **Flying Enterprises**. Air operations started in January 1960 with the Canadair C4 Argonaut. Douglas DC-7s began to arrive in November 1963. The carrier ceased operations in March 1965. Seen on the ramp at Malaga, Spain in August 1964 is OY-DMR Douglas DC-7 (c/n 44140). The aircraft was withdrawn and broken up at Bromma, Sweden in 1968. (KVF)

SAS – Scandinavian Airline System is the multinational airline for Denmark, Norway and Sweden. Set up in 1946, it operates to this day on a world basis. Aeroplanes can be registered in any of the three countries. OY-KNC Douglas DC-7C (c/n 44932) is seen on a passenger charter to Liverpool Speke in June 1964. By this time, many major airlines who still had DC-7s had converted them to cargo operations. The aircraft pictured was sold to French aircraft manufacturer Sud-Est in 1967 and scrapped at Bordeaux in 1980. (KVF)

LEFT:
Once the pinnacle of piston-powered aero engineering, the Douglas DC-7C had a short life at the top because the new generation of jets replaced it on prime routes. Still a good aeroplane, many were converted to cargo operations. This was the fate of pictured **BOAC Cargo** DC-7C G-AOII (c/n 45119). Delivered to Britain's long-haul flag carrier in 1957, it was converted to a cargo carrier in 1960. Sold on to the USA it is still in existence, albeit stored, at Miami. (KVF)

UK carrier **Caledonian Airways** was founded in April 1961 and started flying in November of that year with a flight from London Gatwick to Barbados, using a DC-7 chartered from Sabena. Sadly this aircraft was lost in a fatal crash in Cameroon a few months later. In 1964 the airline was operating low-cost charters to America as well as the usual run of European holiday destinations. It grew to take over British United to become British Caledonian, only to be taken over by British Airways in 1988. Douglas DC-7CG -AOIE (c/n 45115) is seen on the ramp at Palma Majorca in September 1965. This aircraft was stored at Shannon, Ireland in 1970 and then used for rescue training. It is now preserved at Waterford Airport. (KVF)

Like BOAC, **KLM**, the Dutch flag carrier, converted its DC-7s to cargo operations. Seen at Tripoli, Libya in March 1969 is DC-7CF PH-DSG (c/n 45186). Sold on the following month, it ended its days withdrawn and stored at Salisbury Rhodesia (now Harare, Zimbabwe) in 1970. (KVF)

For many ordinary people the only affordable way to the USA in the 1960s was by charter flights. Oakland California-based **Saturn Airways** was a regular visitor to UK airports. Seen at Manchester Ringway in July 1965 is Douglas DC-7C N90773 (c/n 45117) on such a charter. December 1976 saw Saturn merge its identity into TIA (Trans International Airlines). The pictured aircraft was broken up at Miami in 1972. (KVF)

Trans Meridian Air Cargo was a British freight charter operator formed in 1962. Douglas DC-7CF G-ATMF (c/n 44873) is seen at Manchester Ringway in June 1966. The company was renamed British Cargo Airlines in 1979. This aircraft ended its days at Nice where it was broken up in 1972. (KVF)

The German flag carrier **Lufthansa** is among the world's best-known airlines. Post-war operations were resumed in 1955. The airline was one of the operators of the ultimate propliner, the Lockheed L-1649A Starliner. D-ALOL (c/n 1042) is seen here at Frankfurt Rhein Main in June 1962. As with so many of these great piston types, their life span with the major carriers was quite short before being replaced by jets. This Starliner served Lufthansa from 1958 to 1962. It spent most of its subsequent life with Trek Airways of South Africa and has been preserved by the South African Airways museum at Jan Smutts Airport, Johannesburg. (CPW)

Fort Worth Texas-based **American Flyers Airline** flew non-scheduled passenger charters and freight. It frequently flew services for the US military. The company roots go back to a fixed-base operation set up in 1941; it ended following a merger with Universal Airlines in May 1971 with the latter name being used. Seen at Oakland California in April 1965 is the smallest of the Constellations, Lockheed L-049 N88855 (c/n 2055). This model had a wing span of 123ft (37.49m) and a length of 95ft 3in (29.03m). In contrast the L-1649 Starliner had a 150ft (45.72m) span and a 116ft 2in (35.43m) length. This aeroplane was stored at Lancaster California and scrapped in 1971. (CPW)

Luxair, the airline of the Grand Duchy of Luxembourg, operated on behalf of Trek Airways of South Africa, a low-cost flight from Johannesburg using a Lockheed Starliner in Luxair colours. The last leg of the flight was the carrier's own service to London Gatwick. Seen there in August 1968 is LX-LGY Lockheed L-1649A (c/n 1036). This aircraft had a varied career after operating the last Luxair Starliner flight in January 1969, which included serving in the Biafra airlift. It was scrapped at Douala, Cameroon in 1980. (GM)

April 1966 saw the only entry of ACE Freighters into the passenger market. It was then the company founded **ACE Scotland** to operate holiday charters from Glasgow to Mediterranean sunspots. This was a very short-lived operation for, in September of that year, all ACE operations ceased. The ACE Scotland fleet, a single Lockheed L-749A Constellation G-ASYF (c/n 2630) is seen here at Coventry in April 1967. The aircraft was sold and left for Miami where it was scrapped two years later. (IDK)

Euravia was a UK independent, formed with financial backing from several travel companies. Operations started in 1962 with a service from Manchester to Spain. The original fleet consisted of Con-stellations but these were withdrawn during 1965 and replaced by Bristol Britannias. The carrier had also been renamed Britannia Airways. Under this new name it has grown to be one of the largest British holiday operators.

G-AHEN Lockheed L-049 Constellation (c/n 1980) is seen at Liverpool Speke in May 1964. This aircraft was withdrawn from use at Luton in 1965 and broken up the same year. (KVF)

BELOW:
In 1966 England was the host nation for the World Cup soccer trophy. Games were played throughout the country and the city of Liverpool was host to a number of games. Supporters arrived in July in this **Air France** Lockheed L-1049G Super Constellation F-BHBI (c/n 4634). The aircraft, having been converted to a 91 high-density seating configuration, was ideal for such charters. Sold by Air France in 1968, it was used in the Biafra airlift and then stored in the Canary Islands where it was destroyed by fire in 1984. (KVF)

Today that most graceful of aircraft, the Lockheed Constellation, is a very rare sight. Only a few are still airworthy, mainly in the Dominican Republic as cargo aircraft plying their trade around the Caribbean or in America as flying museum aircraft attending airshows. The 1960s was the last decade when a Constellation could be seen in regular service around Europe as a passenger aircraft or in this case a cargo carrier. British independent **ACE** **Freighters** aircraft G-ALAL, an L-749 (c/n 2549), is at Liverpool Speke on 2 July 1966. It has had a problem while off-loading cargo which resulted in it falling back on its tail. The damage was not great and the aircraft was soon upright and back in service. The airline ceased operations two months later. This aircraft flew back to America where it was finally broken up at Miami during 1974. (IDK)

KLM – Royal Dutch Airlines placed an order for twelve Lockheed L-188 Electras in 1956 and received the first in September 1959. The Electra was one of a number of turbine-powered aircraft whose life was cut short by pure jets that had a higher passenger appeal. Most aircraft went on to long and profitable careers with smaller passenger and freight operators. Seen here at Antwerp in June 1962 is PH-LLH Lockheed L-188C Electra (c/n 2015). Note that the tail stripes are at an angle, compare them to the earlier picture of the KLM DC-7. It was thought that the horizontal stripe would be more relaxing for passengers! KLM began selling the Electra fleet with the arrival of DC-9s and the last was disposed of early in 1969. This aircraft is still current today as a cargo aircraft with Hunting Cargo of Dublin. (CPW).

Western Airlines had a history dating back to 1925, making it one of the oldest airlines in America. It ordered nine Electras in 1956 with the first being delivered three years later. Delta Airlines took over the carrier in April 1987. N7142C Lockheed L-188A Electra (c/n 1128) is seen at Calgary Alberta, Canada in June 1967. This aircraft survives to this day and is in store at Coventry UK. (KVF)

Seaboard World Airlines' Canadair CL-44D4-1 N127SW (c/n 27) is seen here at Prestwick Airport in Scotland during August 1964. Seaboard had been founded in 1946 as Seaboard & Western, a scheduled cargo carrier, the current name was adopted in 1961. The airline operated what was then a state-of-the-art cargo aircraft. This design, built in Canada, had been based on the Bristol Britannia but featured a swing tail to ease the loading process. Seaboard merged with Flying Tiger in 1980 and took the latter name. This aircraft was broken up for spare parts in Dallas, Texas during 1980. (IDK)

The Russian design to rival America's Electra and the UK's Britannia was the Ilyushin IL-18 Moskva. First flown in July 1957, it was powered by four Ivchenko AI-20 turboprops of 4000shp (shaft horse power) each. The aircraft had a larger production run than either of its western counterparts. Service life was also longer as 'passenger appeal' was not a phrase in a communist handbook. Most of the airlines of the eastern bloc used the type. Illustrated is SP-LSF (c/n 185008601) of the Polish national carrier **LOT-Polskie Linie Lotnicze** on a service to Zurich in July 1967. This aircraft was sold to Balkan Bulgarian and was reported stored at Varna as late as 1997. (SGW)

Seen at London Gatwick in September 1968 is this Ilyushin IL-18V LZ-BEL (c/n 182004601) of **Bulair**, an affiliate of Balkan Bulgarian. (The name on the cabin roof is in Cyrillic script.) By 1973 the carrier fleet of IL-18/AN12/AN24 had been transferred over to the parent company. The fate of this aircraft is not clear but it is no longer believed to survive. (SGW)

Showing off one of the best colour schemes of the decade is this **British Eagle** BAC 1-11-207AJ G-ATTP (c/n 039) at Liverpool Speke in May 1966. The carrier ran a service from here to London Heathrow. This aircraft ended its days at Santiago, Chile in 1994. (KVF)

Founded in 1966, by one of the great characters of British aviation, Mr Freddie Laker, **Laker Airways** flew holiday charter operations around Europe. G-AVBX BAC 1-11-320AZ (c/n 109) is at London Gatwick in August 1968. The airline suspended services in February 1982 but re-appeared in 1992 as Laker Airways (Bahamas). This aircraft was withdrawn and stored at Benin, Nigeria during 1997. (GM)

Top:
Austrian Airlines bought two 'Dakota replacements' in 1966. These were the British Avro (HS) 748, a turboprop powered by a pair of Rolls-Royce Darts. OE-LHT, a series 2/226 (c/n 1590) is seen arriving at Innsbruck in September 1966. The carrier sold both aircraft within four years. The one pictured was destroyed in an accident at Manila in the Philippines in February 1975. (SGW)

ABOVE:
Skyways Coach Air was a UK holiday company which was in the vanguard of holiday charters, starting in 1955. The 'coach' in the title was because much of the journey was by road. The carrier was taken over by Dan-Air in 1972. G-ARMX

Avro (HS) 748 Series 1/101 (c/n 1538) is seen at a wet Liverpool Speke in May 1965. This aircraft ended its days by being donated to the fire service at Manchester Ringway in 1990 where it still survives, albeit in a poor condition. (KVF)

ABOVE:
Air Ceylon used to be the flag carrier for that island state. It was re-named Sri Lanka following independence from the UK. This airline suspended services at the end of the 1970s. Seen here is 4R-ACN de Havilland DH-121 Trident 1E-140 (c/n 2135) at Paris Le Bourget in June 1969 as an exhibit at the Paris Air Show, prior to delivery. The aircraft was used until 1978 and then became a ground trainer before being scrapped in 1998. (SGW)

BELOW:
BEA – British European Airways had the Trident designed to its requirements and was the type's major user. Seen in June 1967 at London Heathrow is a row of four, with G-ARPU de Havilland DH-121 Trident 1C (c/n 2120) at the front. This aircraft was destroyed by fire whilst parked at this airport in July 1969. (CPW)

The last design from the Airspeed company was the AS57 Ambassador. Power was provided by two Bristol Centaurus radial piston engines of 2700hp each. This example was operated by British independent **Dan-Air**. It is seen on the ramp at Manchester Ringway in August 1964. G-ALZX (c/n 5220) was damaged beyond economic repair in a landing accident at Beauvais, France in April 1966. (IDK)

British independent Autair leased this Airspeed AS57 Ambassador G-ALZZ (c/n 5222) to **Skyways Coach Air** for four months during 1968. It is seen at London Gatwick in August of that year. The following year it was withdrawn and broken up at Luton. (GM)

ABOVE:

BKS Air Transport was started in 1952, the name being derived from three directors' names, Barnby/Keegan/Stevens, The Bloodstock and Cargo division was founded in 1967 at Belfast. It was this unit's task to fly race horses around Europe. In November 1970 the carrier changed its name to Northeast Airlines. G-ALZR Airspeed AS57 Ambassador (c/n 5214) is at Liverpool Speke in March 1968. In July the following year it was damaged beyond economic repair when the nose wheel collapsed whilst landing at London Gatwick. Sold to Dan-Air for spares, it was broken-up at Lasham in 1972. (KVF)

BELOW:

1953 was the year UK independent **Autair** was formed as a helicopter company. Dakotas were added to the fleet in 1960 and the following year they began I/T operations. The fleet included such types as Viking/Bristol Freighter/Skymaster/ Herald. Pictured is Airspeed AS57 Ambassador G-ALZV (c/n 5218) at Liverpool Speke in January 1965. The carrier operated three of these aircraft between 1963 and 1969. This aircraft was scrapped at Luton during 1968. The airline changed its name to Court Line at the start of 1970. (KVF)

The last of the four Vickers VC10s operated by **British United** was the prototype. First flown in 1962, it joined the fleet in April 1969. G-ARTA (c/n 803) is seen the following month at its London Gatwick base. VC10s were used for scheduled services to South America. Following a heavy landing at base in January 1972 this aircraft was withdrawn and scrapped. (KVF)

The British long-haul flag carrier, BOAC, had the VC10 designed for its empire routes. It was able to operate from hot, high and short runways. This design process took place in the 1950s. By the time the aircraft was in service in 1964 the empire had shrunk, and those newly independent countries had built long runways able to take any jet. Seen here is G-ASGB Vickers 1151 Super VC10 (c/n 852) at New York – JFK in September 1965. The Super VC10 was the only major model change. It was 13ft (3.96m) longer, and had greater fuel capacity and more powerful Rolls-Royce Conway engines. The aircraft illustrated has the name **BOAC-Cunard**, which refers to an operating agreement that existed from 1962 until 1966 when the Cunard Shipping Line had a 30% to 70% BOAC business split on the north Atlantic route. The aircraft's fate was to be sold to the Royal Air Force in 1981 and then broken up at RAF Abingdon in 1987. (CPW)

Belgium's national airline **Sabena** (Société Anonyme Belge d'Exploitation de la Navigation Aérienne) has a history dating back to 1923. From its Brussels base it operates worldwide with the latest Airbus A340s. OO-SJE Boeing 707-329 (c/n 17627) is seen on a charter to Liverpool Speke in June 1968. This aircraft was destroyed in a crash at Tenerife in February 1978. (KVF)

This Boeing 707 was the last aircraft to enter service with **British Eagle**. It joined the fleet in March 1968 and later that year, in November, the carrier ceased flying. G-AWDG Boeing 707-138B (c/n 17702) is seen at London Gatwick in February 1969 following the airline's demise. In the first instance it went to Laker and then began a new life as an executive jet. In this role it continues to this day. (KVF)

BOAC – British Overseas Airways Corporation was Britain's state-owned long-haul flag carrier. Following the 1974 forced merger with BEA it became British Airways. G-APFG Boeing 707-436 (c/n 17708) is seen at Manchester Ringway in August 1964, operating a scheduled service to New York. The airframe was withdrawn from use in 1981 and used as a maintenance trainer at Stansted. In 1989 the fuselage was used for trials of fire equipment at Cardington where it still survives. (IDK)

The short-bodied Boeing 720 had a production run of just 154 from 1960 to 1967. This derivative of the more famous 707 was designed for short to medium routes. AP-AMG, a 720-040B (c/n 18378) is seen here in the colours of Pakistan International Airlines, the government-owned flag carrier, at London Heathrow in September 1968. The airline is still, of course, current but this aeroplane was used for fire practice at Luqa, Malta following its withdrawal from service with Air Malta. This carrier had bought the aircraft from PIA. (IDK)

ABOVE:

America's **United Airlines** has grown from being a major domestic carrier in the 1960s to its role today as one of the world's biggest operators. It adopted the name following a multi-airline merger in 1931. Boeing 720-022 N7221U (c/n 18074) is seen in November 1966 at Vancouver British Columbia. It is of note that this aircraft lacks the HF (High Frequency) Antenna on the top of the fin. This is due to the fact that most of the airline's operations were over the continental USA and that the new VHF (Very High Frequency) communications system was in place by spring 1960. Airlines such as Aer Lingus who flew over long stretches of water still needed the HF antenna, as do most 707s. This airframe ended its days being scrapped at Miami in 1983. (KVF)

ABOVE:

Saudi Arabian Airlines is that nation's flag carrier. Government-owned, it is based in the capital Jeddah. Its large and modern fleet has been built up on the country's vast oil wealth. HZ-ACA Boeing 720-060B (c/n 18165) is seen at Tripoli, Libya in March 1969. Sold on, it ended its days being broken up at Moses Lake, Washington in 1982. (KVF)

World Airways was formed in 1948 as a non-scheduled carrier. It has grown to this day to have a large fleet of DC-10/MD11 wide-bodies. N375WA Boeing 707-373C (c/n 18707) is seen at London Gatwick in August 1969. Sold on to a number of operators, it was destroyed in a take-off crash at Medellin, Colombia in December 1983. (SGW)

Pacific Western Airlines of Vancouver British Columbia flew an extensive network of scheduled passenger services around the western provinces of Canada and across into the USA. The carrier was merged into Canadian in April 1987. Seen at Manchester Ringway, in September 1969, is CF-PWV Boeing 707-138 (c/n 17696) on a transatlantic charter. This aircraft still operates today as an executive jet owned by the government of Saudi Arabia. (SGW)

Universal Airlines was formed in 1966 following a take over of Zantop Air Transport, not to be confused with the later Zantop International Airlines. In the early days it flew mainly cargo for the automobile industry as its base was Willow Run, Detroit. Jets were acquired so the company could move into long-haul charters. Operations ceased in 1972 with the company going into bankruptcy. N802U Douglas DC-8-61CF (c/n 45950) is seen at London Gatwick, September 1969. This aircraft has been re-engined with CFM56s, thus making it a series 71 and today is operated by United Parcel Service. (SGW)

ABOVE:
Saturn Airways switched to jets for its transatlantic charter services during the sixties. N3325T Douglas DC-8-55 (c/n 45754) is at London Gatwick in August 1969. This aircraft crashed after take off at Quito, Ecuador in September 1984. (SGW)

BELOW:
This Douglas DC-8-52 OB-R-931 (c/n 45619) of **APSA – Aerolineas Peruanas** is on lease from Iberia. It operated a scheduled service to London Gatwick where it is seen in August 1969. APSA got into financial difficulties and ceased operations in May 1971. The aeroplane was sold on and scrapped at Miami during 1990. (SGW)

New York-based **ONA – Overseas National Airways** flew both passenger and cargo operations following its formation in 1950. The US military were frequent customers. Operations were suspended in September 1978. Seen on a charter to London Gatwick in August 1969 is N852F Douglas DC-8-55F (c/n 45856). The aircraft is still in operation today as a freighter in the USA. (SGW)

During the 1960s few domestic American airlines were to be seen in Europe except on charter or trooping flights. Scheduled services were the domain of the twin flag carriers Pan Am and TWA. Seen at Prestwick, Scotland in May 1967 is Texas-based **Braniff International** Douglas DC-8-55F N1509U (c/n 45858). The airline was one of the casualties of the 1979 American airline deregulation. It has made a number of comebacks but no longer operates. This aircraft was sold on to many different countries and operators, its last role being as a freighter with Flash Airlines of Nigeria. This carrier ceased operations during October 1995 and the aircraft is listed as stored. (IDK)

ABOVE:
The Convair liner was one of the more successful post-war piston-engined airliners. There were three basic models, the 240/340/440. Many had their Pratt & Whitney R2800 radial pistons replaced by Allison 501 or Rolls-Royce Dart turboprops making them 580 and 600 models. **Swissair** bought its first four 240s in 1949 and operated a total of over twenty of all models. HB-IMR Convair CV440 (c/n 429) is seen at Hanover in May 1964. This aircraft was sold on to various operators and destroyed in a crash at Trieste, Yugoslavia in December 1971. (CPW)

BELOW:
Belgian flag carrier **Sabena** has been running a scheduled service to Manchester Ringway for many years. In August 1964 it was being run with this Convair CV440 OO-SCP (c/n 367). This was powered by two 2500hp Pratt & Whitney R2800 radial piston engines and had a maximum speed of 310mph (499kph). Bought new by Sabena in 1956, it served until 1968 when it was sold in America. Here it was re-engined with Allison 501 turboprops of 3750shp (shaft horse power). At the current time the aircraft is still in operation with the Bolivian Air Force at La Paz. (IDK)

ABOVE:
Spanish flag carrier **Iberia** operated a total of seventeen Convairs between 1957 and 1972. EC-AMR CV440 (c/n 401) is at Malaga in August 1964. It was sold on to, first, the Spanish Air Force and then to Mexico, and finally the USA where it was probably used for spares. (KVF)

BELOW:
When **Lufthansa** resumed post-war operations the first aircraft to serve was the Convair liner. These flew the European routes until replaced by Viscounts. D-ACOH Convair CV340 (converted to 440) (c/n 213) is seen at Hanover in May 1964. Sold on by Lufthansa, it had many owners before being stored at Carlsbad California and scrapped in the early 1990s. (CPW)

Allegheny Airlines was a large domestic scheduled passenger carrier operating in the north-eastern corner of America. It had one experience with the Convair liner that is of note, being the launch customer for the British Napier Eland turboprop version, the 540. Rolls-Royce bought Napier and cancelled the engine which meant that turboprops were converted back to piston power. N3415 Convair CV340 (c/n 46) is seen at Trumbull Airport, Groton Connecticut in November 1965. After it was sold on this airframe was fitted with Allison turboprops making it a CV580 and it is still current in Canada. Allegheny, at the end of the 1970s, became US Airways. (CPW)

The de Havilland Heron was a development of the DH-104 Dove, being enlarged and with four 250hp de Havilland Gipsy Queen piston engines. It was first flown in May 1950. They were used as small airliners and as executive transports. In Britain the Queen's Flight of the Royal Air Force operated two of the designs. OO-BIA DH-114 Heron 1B (c/n 14043) is in the colours of **Sabena** and carries the title 'Common Market Commuter'. The Common Market was the name for what we know now as the European Union. It is pictured at a snow-covered Rotterdam in January 1968. Sold on, the aircraft was broken up for scrap at Southend, UK in 1972. (KVF)

Mercury Airlines was a British charter carrier who used that name from 1961. By the time it ceased operations in October 1964 it had started a number of scheduled domestic passenger services. G-AOZN de Havilland DH-114 Heron 1B (c/n 14005) is at Liverpool Speke in June 1964. It is of note that the mark 1 of the Heron had a fixed undercarriage. The mark 2 had a retractable one resulting in a higher (20mph/32.18kph) speed and better fuel economy due to less drag. This aircraft was sold on and ended its days in New Zealand, where it was damaged beyond economic repair in May 1977. (KVF)

The Aviation Traders' Carvair was developed to be a successor to the Bristol Freighter, especially in the long-haul, into middle Europe, market. The idea came from Mr Freddie Laker, then the Managing Director of Air Charter, who suggested using a DC-4 with its nose cut off just ahead of the wing with a totally new nose fitted, featuring a front loading cargo door.

This new design was able to carry five cars and their full passenger load. G-AOFW ATL98 Carvair (c/n 12/10351) is seen at Liverpool Speke, September 1965, in the colours of **British United Air Ferries**. The carrier later changed the name of this division to British Air Ferries (BAF). The pictured aircraft was broken up at Southend, UK in 1983. (KVF)

Spanish carrier **Aviaco**, a subsidiary of Iberia, operated a total of three Carvairs, the name of the type being derived from 'Car via Air'. They were used on services between Palma Majorca to Barcelona and Valencia. This service carrying cars ran from 1964 until 1968. Seen on the ramp at Palma, September 1965, is ATL98 Carvair EC-AZA (c/n 18/18340). Sold on in 1969, it ended its days in the Dominican Republic where it was scrapped in the late 1970s. (KVF)

ABOVE:
The Irish national airline **Aer Lingus** operated a fleet of three new Carvairs on services across the Irish Sea. Seen at one of the UK served destinations, Liverpool Speke, in April 1964 is EI-ANJ ATL98 (c/n 14/10458). The service ended in 1966 due to competition from 'drive on' car ferry ships. This aircraft was sold on first to Canada and ended its days being scrapped at Bangkok, Thailand. (KVF)

One of the shortest operations of the Carvair was that of **Alisud** (Compagnia Aerea Meridionale), which flew a daily service between Naples and Palermo in Sicily. The route was first flown in August 1963 using a leased BUAF aircraft, and ceased in February the following year. G-ASKG ATL98 Carvair (c/n 10/10382) is seen back at Southend in March 1964 following the lease. This aircraft went on to have a number of owners and was eventually scrapped in 1995 at Kinshasa, Republic of Congo. (KVF)

The Curtiss C-46 Commando is one of the greatest work-horse props of the world, a tramp steamer of the skies. It is not a sight to be seen in Europe now, as none can be found in service, nor even in a museum. To see one in operation you have to go to places such as Alaska, Bolivia or Colombia. Seen here is N10427 C-46A Commando (c/n 30532) of **Seaboard World Airlines** at Frankfurt, December 1967. This long-established carrier used a number of locally based C-46s to ferry around European destinations,cargo that had been brought over from America by its CL-44 or DC-8 fleet. Sold on, this aircraft crashed in Colombia in February 1973. (KVF)

The Boeing 727 was and continues to be used worldwide for both passenger and freight operations. It was first flown in February 1963. Seen on the ramp at Toronto Ontario, September 1969, is **United Airlines** Boeing 727-22 N7049U (c/n 18856). This early short-bodied aircraft was sold on and destroyed in a take-off crash in Costa Rica in May 1988. (KVF)

ABOVE:
US carrier **American Flyers** operated this Boeing 727-185 N12826 (c/n 19826) on transatlantic charter operations. It is seen at London Gatwick in June 1969. This aircraft can still be found in service today with freight operator UPS (United Parcel Service). This carrier has extended the life of many of its aircraft, including this one, by replacing the original Pratt & Whitney JT8D engines with three Rolls-Royce Tay 651-54 units. Aircraft converted this way have the letters 'QF' added to their designation to indicate they are now 'Quiet Freighters'. (KVF)

BELOW:
Germany's **Lufthansa** was an early customer of the Boeing 727, they first operated the short-bodied 100 series and later bought the longer, by 20 feet (6.09 m), 200 series. Seen here on the ramp at Palma Majorca in September 1965 is D-ABIL Boeing 727-30 (c/n 18367). Sold on, this aircraft is currently stored in the Republic of Congo. (KVF)

The Bristol 170 Freighter was first flown in December 1945 as a general freighter with large nose doors to allow easy loading of cargo or vehicles. The type inaugurated a car ferry service from Lympne Kent to Le Touquet France in 1948. It was for this service that the aircraft was most famous. Seen here at Liverpool Speke in November 1964 is **BKS Air Transport** Bristol 170 Freighter Mk31E G-AMLJ (c/n 13072). It was used to operate a car ferry service to Dublin with two cars and their passengers. This aircraft was sold to Aer Turas and then ended its days being scrapped at Nice in 1976. (KVF)

Irish independent **Aer Turas** started operations in 1962 with a de Havilland DH-89 Dragon Rapide. By May 1966 the fleet mix had included DC-3/DC-4 and this Bristol 170 Freighter Mk31E EI-APC (c/n 13072). The aeroplane was used for general cargo and most especially the carriage of blood stock race horses. Eagle-eyed readers will spot that this is the same aircraft as shown in the BKS picture. (KVF)

ABOVE:
French car ferry operator **Cie (Compagnie) Air Transport** operated a service from both Le Touquet and Calais to Lydd (Kent) in conjunction with BUAF. The aircraft that operated this was the long-nosed Mark 32 Super Freighter. The extra 5 feet (1.52 m) length enabled a third car to be carried. Making a rare visit to Liverpool Speke in November 1967 is F-BKBI Bristol Super Freighter Mk32 (c/n 13213). It was withdrawn from service three months later and scrapped later in 1968. It is sad to report that there are no Super Freighters left in the world. Several of the short-nosed Mk31 are still to be found in service as well as preserved examples but not its bigger brother. (IDK)

BELOW:
Seen in its final operating colour scheme is G-ANVR Bristol 170 Super Freighter Mk32 (c/n 13251) of **BUAF – British United Air Ferries** at Liverpool Speke in October 1967. The type and operator were usually seen plying across the English Channel with its two Bristol 1675hp Hercules radial pistons pounding away. The type was one where both airframe and power-plant were manufactured by the same company. This aircraft was one of the last Super Freighters in service, with Midland Air Cargo, and was scrapped at Coventry, UK in 1974. (KVF)

When an early short DC-9 is seen today it looks like one of the bigger biz-jets. The aeroplane has been stretched to an almost incredible length. From 105ft 5in (32.13m) for the DC-9-10 to 152ft 7in (46.5m) for a current MD-90 and able to carry twice the passenger load. Seen on the ramp at London Gatwick, August 1969, is D-AMOR Douglas DC-9-15 (c/n 45787) named 'Lovebird', a most suitable name for that registration. The operator **Germanair** was an independent charter company which was taken over by Transportflug in 1969. This aircraft is still in service today with the large American airline Northwest. (KVF)

BELOW:
In the early days of its type operation DC-9 freighters were not that common. Seen at Tripoli, Libya in March 1969 is Italian flag carrier **Alitalia** Douglas DC-9-32F I-DIKG (c/n 47221) showing off a very distinctive 'Cargo System' colour scheme. This aircraft was sold on and is currently operated by the US Navy. (KVF)

A picture that might well be captioned deux Deux Ponts, as it shows two of the Breguet 763 Deux Ponts (Double Decker) at Marseille Marignane in August 1964. This French transport was powered by four American Pratt & Whitney R2800 radial piston engines of 1927hp. As the name suggests it carried passengers on two decks or, in many cases, the bottom deck was used for cargo. Only twelve production aircraft were built for the national carrier **Air France**, and a number were later transferred to the French Air Force (Armée de l'Air). This aircraft F-BASU (c/n 8) was withdrawn from use in 1970 and scrapped at Paris Orly. (CPW)

The Vickers Viking was one of the first British attempts in the post-war period to restart building transport aircraft. During World War II they had built only combat aircraft and had allowed America to forge ahead in the design and production of commercial aircraft. The Viking was based upon parts from the Wellington bomber and was powered by a pair of well-proven Bristol Hercules engines. Sold to BEA from the manufacturer, it found favour among many charter operators. Seen at Liverpool Speke in December 1965 is G-AHPL Vickers Viking 1B (c/n 149) of UK independent **Invicta**. This aircraft was withdrawn from use in 1967 and scrapped. (KVF)

ABOVE:
British charter carrier **Air Ferry** flew a total of five Vikings between February 1962 and November 1966. Seen at Liverpool Speke in November 1964 is G-AIVF Vickers Viking 1B (c/n 219). Sold on, it ended its days withdrawn and scrapped at Manston, Kent during 1969. (KVF)

BELOW:
Braathens SAFE (South American and Far East Air Transport) was founded in 1946 by the family of the same name. It also ran a shipping line and used the original fleet of four Douglas Skymasters for flights between Oslo and Hong Kong with ship's crews during the early days of operation.

Other charter work soon grew, as did scheduled passenger services. The airline still exists today and has a fleet of 40+ Boeing 737s. Seen at Liverpool Speke in April 1964 is Fokker F27 Friendship 100 LN-SUE (c/n 10245). Sold on, this aircraft was withdrawn and stored in 1996. (KVF)

One of the more successful aircraft designed to be a 'Dakota replacement' was the Dutch-designed Fokker F27 Friendship. First flown in 1955 it proved to be a popular type, powered by a pair of Rolls-Royce Dart turboprops. Friendships entered service with **Aer Lingus** in December 1958 on the route from Dublin to Liverpool. EI-AKB Friendship 100 (c/n 10106) is seen on a night service to the latter location in March 1964. Sold on, it had a long career and was eventually withdrawn during 1996 and used for fire practice at Västeräs, Sweden. (IDK)

Fairchild, in the United States, ran a parallel F27 production plant to the Amsterdam factory. Seen at Spokane Washington in April 1967 is Fairchild F27 Friendship N2708 (c/n 24) of **West Coast Airlines**. This carrier was certified and operated its first service in 1946 with a DC-3 flying between Seattle Washington and Portland Oregon. The airline operated the world's first F27 service on 27 September 1958. This preceded any Fokker-built aircraft by several months. In April 1968 the operator merged with Bonanza and Pacific to form Air West. This aircraft has now ended its flying days and is an instructional airframe in New Zealand. (KVF)

Dutch carrier **Schreiner Airways** was first formed in 1945 and flew charters. It is still in operation today, flying scheduled services with a fleet of de Havilland (Canada) DHC-8 Dash 8s. Seen on a charter flight to Liverpool Speke in June 1966 is Fokker F27 Friendship 100 PH-SAP (c/n 10107). Sold on to a number of other carriers, it was withdrawn and stored in The Gambia during 1996. (KVF)

Formed in 1964, **Kingdom of Libya Airlines** began operations the following year. Seen on the ramp at Sebha in February 1969 is I-ATIM Fokker F27 Friendship 200 (c/n 10249). The Italian registration is because it was on lease from Aero Transporti Italiani. This aircraft is still in operation today. The airline was renamed Libyan Arab Airlines following the September 1969 revolution. (KVF)

ABOVE:
Dominie Airways was a subsidiary company of British independent, Treffield. It flew one aircraft, this de Havilland DH-89A Dragon Rapide G-AHKU (c/n 6810). The airline's name was derived from the military title for the type. It was used for ad hoc charters and pleasure flying. The operator ceased trading when the parent company folded in 1967. G-AHKU is pictured at East Midlands – Castle Donnington in March 1967. The aircraft was withdrawn from use in August 1970. (IDK)

BELOW:
The Martin 404 was derived from the model 202. As a post-war airliner it was head-to-head in competition for sales with the Convair range. Both types had a similar outline shape. The 404 was powered by two Pratt & Whitney R2800 radial piston engines of 2400hp. The biggest users were Eastern and TWA who had a fleet of 100 between them. Seen at Ventura County Airport California in April 1965 is N455A Martin 404 (c/n 14146) of **Pacific Air Lines**. This San Francisco-based carrier had adopted the name in 1958 and was one of the three airlines who formed Air West in April 1968. This aircraft was sold on to a number of operators and ended its days in Bolivia. (CPW)

RIGHT:

Pan American World Airways was perhaps the best-known carrier in the world for many years. It was a sad day for aviation history when in December 1991, following mounting losses, the airline ceased operations. A new company has since revived the name. The 1960s was one of its busiest periods. As well as world-wide services with the Boeing 707, it also operated internal German passenger flights. The Four Powers Agreement at the end of World War II had decreed that services to Berlin could only be run by British, French or US airlines. This meant that when Lufthansa was reformed in the 1950s it was not allowed to fly to that divided city. Seen at Hanover in May 1964 is N6526C Douglas DC-6B (c/n 43526) operating an internal service. This aircraft ended its days when it crashed in Brazil in April 1972 whilst operating for a Panamanian airline. (KVF)

Before its break-up in civil war, Yugoslavia was a popular holiday destination for many people. During the 1960s **Adria Airlines** of Ljubljana operated five Douglas DC-6Bs to fly holidaymakers from their local airport for two weeks of sunshine. YU-AFE (c/n 43552) is at Manchester Ringway in August 1964. The airline still operates today but as part of the newly independent country of Slovenia. The aircraft ended its days with an Icelandic cargo airline before being withdrawn from use and broken up at Keflavik in 1975. (IDK)

Finnish operator **Kar-Air** was founded in 1957. It flew both scheduled and charter work and was owned by national flag carrier Finnair. Seen at London Gatwick on a holiday charter, August 1969, is OH-KDC Douglas DC-6B (c/n 44169). Sold on, it was destroyed by fire at Antwerp, Belgium in January 1974. (SGW)

Belgian flag carrier **Sabena** operated this Douglas DC-6B OO-CTM (c/n 44175) from new in January 1954 until they sold it to the Luftwaffe eleven years later. Its latter use with Sabena was to operate charters as piston-power was not popular with passengers flying with national carriers. Seen at Liverpool Speke in November 1964, it was bringing in the football supporters for the Belgian team Anderlecht. This aeroplane is still in existence today at Kinshasa, Republic of Congo. (KVF)

BIAS – Belgian International Air Services
was founded in 1959 with a single Douglas
Skymaster for charter work. The crisis in
the former Belgian Congo during 1961 had
the company working flat out with its
fleet, now doubled, on relief missions.
European I/T and charter work grew with
the acquisition of a pair of DC-6s in 1962.
The company ceased trading in 1980. Seen
in September 1966 at Manchester Ringway
is OO-GER Douglas DC-6B (c/n 43826).
Sold on to various African states, it was
withdrawn and stored at Niamey, Niger in
1981. (KVF)

The colours of Norwegian independent, **Braathens SAFE**, were a common sight at European holiday destinations. Seen flying tourists to the sun from London Gatwick in August 1968 is Douglas DC-6B LN-SUM (c/n 45079). The carrier sold this aircraft the following year and it ended its days in the Yemen. (GM)

LEFT:
Seen at Toronto International in June 1967 is CF-PWF Douglas DC-6B (c/n 43537) of **Pacific Western Airlines** disgorging its predominantly business passengers. The carrier was based in Vancouver British Columbia and flew an extensive service of scheduled passenger flights around the western provinces of Canada and into the USA. It merged into the current airline, Canadian, in April 1987. This aircraft ended its days as a tanker for Conair of Abbotsford British Columbia, fighting forest fires. It was withdrawn from service and used for spares before finally being scrapped. (KVF)

BELOW:
The national flag carrier of Iceland is **Icelandair**. Scheduled services are flown east to Europe and west to the USA from its mid-Atlantic location. Seen at Liverpool Speke in September 1964 is TF-ISC Douglas DC-6B (c/n 43744). Sold on in 1973, it was converted to cargo configuration and was eventually scrapped in Cyprus in 1995. (KVF)

RIGHT:
Douglas DC-6B I-DIME (c/n 44252) of Italian holiday charter operator **SAM – Societa Aerea Mediterranea** is seen at Manchester Ringway in August 1964. This carrier was merged with its parent company, Alitalia, during 1974. The aeroplane was sold on to the Italian Air Force who operated it from 1970 to 1974 when it was withdrawn from service. (IDK)

BELOW:
Canadian Pacific had a history going back to 1942 when the railway company of the same name acquired a number of small bush operators and amalgamated their services. From 1968 it was known as CP Air and in April 1987 it merged with Pacific Western to form Canadian. Douglas DC-6B CF-CUS (c/n 45178) is seen on a domestic service to Penticton British Columbia in January 1967. This aircraft was converted to a freighter at the end of the decade and passed through a number of operators before being scrapped at Miami in 1993. (KVF)

British Midland is one of the leading UK airlines for domestic and European passenger services. Based at East Midlands – Castle Donnington, its first turboprop was this Handley Page HPR-7 Herald 211 G-ASKK (c/n 161). It was introduced in February 1965 and is pictured at base two months later. This aircraft has since been preserved at the City of Norwich Aviation Museum in Norfolk UK. (IDK)

The Handley Page HPR-7 Herald was one of a number of 1960s 'Dakota replacements', however only fifty were manufactured. At the time of writing the number of operational Heralds is down to a single figure. Seen at Liverpool Speke in April 1967 is G-APWC (c/n 151) of **Autair**, a UK charter operator. This aircraft was sold on to Colombia where it was withdrawn from use in 1976 at Villiavicencio and scrapped in 1992. This is ironic, for today this airfield has one of the highest and healthiest populations of working Dakotas in the world. (IDK)

ABOVE:

South West Aviation was a UK independent airline based at Exeter. Formed in 1966, it flew charters and scheduled passenger flights with a variety of aircraft types. In 1972 the company was bought and moved location, the name no longer being used. Pictured is Short SC.7 Skyvan 2 G-ATPF (c/n SH1833) at Liverpool Speke in May 1968. This design was a bid to capture the market for a simple freight aircraft. It was loaded by a large rear fuselage door. Early aircraft were powered by a pair of Turbomeca Astazou turboprops of 690shp. This powerplant had problems in hot and high locations. The series 3 aircraft were fitted with Garrett AiResearch TP331 units of 715shp. This aircraft was withdrawn by the manufacturer, who had owned it all its life, mainly leasing it to various carriers. It was scrapped in 1976. (IDK)

BELOW:

The Canadair C4 was a licensed-built DC-4 fitted with four Rolls-Royce Merlin liquid cooled piston engines of 1760hp each. In addition to the engine change the other major difference from the Douglas-built airframes was that the fuselage was pressurised. Known as the Argonaut in service with BOAC, it was from this source that UK operator's aircraft came. Seen at Liverpool Speke in February 1965 is G-ALHG (c/n 153) of **British Midland**. In October the previous year it had changed its name from Derby Airways. This aircraft crashed at Stockport on approach to Manchester Ringway in June 1967 and was destroyed. (KVF)

RIGHT:
British independent **Air Links** first operated in 1959 and flew charter operations, first with Dakotas and then with the Handley Page Hermes. The carrier operated the last commercial service of that aircraft type. Seen at Liverpool Speke in September 1965 is Canadair C4 Argonaut G-ALHI (c/n 155). The airline was, by the start of that year, an all C4 operator and the previous month had changed its name to Transglobe. This aircraft was withdrawn in November 1965 and ended its days at the fire school at Stansted. (KVF)

BELOW:
The flag carrier for the African republic of Ghana is **Ghana Airways**, which currently operates a pair of DC-9s and DC-10s for domestic and international services. They bought this Bristol Britannia 309 G-ANCH (c/n 12924) in August 1960. It spent much of its life on lease to other companies. It is seen at Liverpool Speke in March 1968 during a spell with British Eagle. It was retired in 1972 and broken up at Biggin Hill, Kent the following year. (KVF)

UK independent **Transglobe** flew the usual mix of ad hoc charters and holiday flights taking sunseekers to Mediterranean beaches. G-ATGD Bristol Britannia 314 (c/n 13393) is at Palma Majorca in September 1965. The airline ceased operations in November 1969 following financial problems. This aircraft was sold on and was scrapped at Biggin Hill, Kent in 1971. (KVF)

Lloyd International Airways was founded in 1961 by two shipping brokers, one of them, Brian Lloyd, giving his name to the company. The plan for operation of the first aircraft, a Douglas Skymaster, was to fly ships' crews and cargo from the UK to the Far East. Other charter work was added to utilise the aeroplane. Bristol Britannias were added to the fleet in 1965. The carrier ceased trading in June 1972. Seen at Liverpool Speke in November 1967 is G-AOVP Bristol Britannia 312 (c/n 13424) in its new guise as a converted freighter. It was withdrawn from use in 1975 at Biggin Hill, Kent and scrapped. (KVF)

The Bristol 175 Britannia or 'Whispering Giant' as she became known, was first flown in August 1952 from the maker's base at Filton. The launch customer was the British long-haul, government-owned, flag carrier **BOAC – British Overseas Airways Corporation**. Seen at Prestwick in June 1963 is BOAC Britannia 312 G-AOVJ (c/n 13418). The 300 series was a stretched version from the original 100 and had a longer range. The design was powered by four Bristol Proteus turboprops. This aircraft was sold on and ended its days at the fire school at Stansted. (IDK)

Up to the time of the carrier's demise in November 1968, **British Eagle** had operated, leased, and owned twenty-three different Britannias, but not all at the same time. This figure was second only to that of BOAC. Seen at Liverpool Speke in April 1964 is Bristol Britannia 312 G-AOVM (c/n 13421). This aircraft flew later for a number of operators and ended its days in Africa where it was broken up for spares at Kinshasa, Republic of Congo during 1994. (KVF)

ABOVE:

African Safari Airways had a short life. It was formed in November 1967 by staff from the collapsed Globe Air, and suspended operations in 1971 (another company now operates services using this name and currently operates a single DC-10.) The carrier's prime business was to fly tourists from Switzerland to East Africa for safari holidays. Other destinations soon followed. Seen at London Gatwick in May 1969 is Bristol Britannia 313 5X-UVH (c/n 13431). This aircraft was retired in May 1975 at Stansted UK. Like so many other aircraft at that location it was used by the fire-fighting school. (KVF)

RIGHT:

Owned by one of the biggest tour companies, Thomsons, **Britannia Airways** is today one of Britain's leading holiday charter airlines with a fleet of Boeing 757 and 767s. These aircraft can be seen on both long and short-haul flights. The company took the present name when it began to operate the Britannia in 1964, prior to this it had been known as Euravia. Seen at Liverpool Speke in May 1965 is Bristol Britannia 102 G-ANBO (c/n 12916), this aircraft was retired in 1970 and broken up at Luton the following year. (KVF)

Founded in 1965 by Freddie Laker with two Britannias, **Laker Airways** operated these aircraft on ad hoc charters and leases to other carriers. They were both replaced by jets after a few years of service. G-ANBM Bristol Britannia 102 (c/n 12914) is at Liverpool Speke in June 1968. It was sold on to Indonesia where it was withdrawn from use during 1970 and broken up at Jakarta the following year. (KVF)

Bibliography

Chillton, J. : Dubois, J.P. : Wegg, J.
French Post-war Transport Aircraft
Air Britain 1980

Eastwood, Tony and Roach, John
Piston Engine Airliner Production List 1996
Jet Airliner Production List 1998
Turbo Prop Airliner Production List 1998
The Aviation Hobby Shop

Horan, V.
Survivors 97
Gatwick Aviation Society 1997

Powers, D.G.
Lockheed L188 Electra
World Transport Press 1999

Waddington, T.
Douglas DC-8
World Transport Press 1996

Lo Bao, P.
Bristol Britannia
Aviation Data Centre 1996

Gradidge, J.M.
The Douglas DC-3
The Convairliners Story
Air Britain 1984 & 1998

Davis, J.M. : Martin, H.G. : Whittle, J.A.
The Curtiss C46 Commando
Air Britain 1978

Marson, P.J.
The Lockheed Constellation Series
Air Britain 1982

Merton Jones, A.C.
British Independent Airlines since 1946
MAS/LAAS 1976

Klee, U.
JP Airline Fleets
Buchair (Various editions)

Magazines

Airliners – various editions
Propliner – various editions